POEM RUNS

Baseball Poems and Paintings by

Douglas Florian

HARCOURT CHILDREN'S BOOKS

Houghton Mifflin Harcourt

Boston   New York   2012

In blessed memory of my father,

Harold Florian

CONTENTS

Warm Up	4
Play Ball!	5
Pitcher	6
Catcher	9
Our Slugger	10
A Baseball	12
First Baseman	15
Base Stealer	17
Right Fielder	18
Umpire	21
Second Baseman	22
Shortstop	25
Third Baseman	27
Poem Run	29
The Season Is Over	30

WARM UP

Bend to the left.

       Bend to the right.

S t r e t c h out those muscles,

Too tense and too tight.

Catch a ball lightly.

Jump up and jog.

Warm yourself up

Like a fireplace log.

PLAY BALL!

The winter is through.
    The springtime is here.
The season is new.
    The weather is clear.
We're ready to hit one
    Right over the wall.
The winter is through—
    Throw out the first ball!

PITCHER

I'm the curve-ball creator,
The man on the mound.
The great devastator,
Where fastballs are found.

I'm the slippery slider.
My sinker just p
          l
            u
              m
                m
                  e
                    t
                      s.

I'm sly as a spider.

                s summits.
              b
            m
          i
        l
My riser c

I'm the scourge of all hitters,
The starter of slumps.
I make batters bitter,
Turn bats into stumps.

I'm the strikeout collector.
You'll only hit air.
The slim-lead protector—
Beware! Beware!

CATCHER

I can catch curve balls.
I can catch heat.
I can catch sliders
With glove or with feet.

I block with my belly.
I nab with my knees.
Throw me jars of jelly.
I'll grab them with ease.

Throw screwballs,
Or two balls,
Brand-new balls—
I'll snatch 'em.

Throw low-balls,
Big snowballs,
Or cannonballs—
I'll catch 'em!

OUR SLUGGER

Our slugger is strong.
    Our slugger is mean,
With arms very long
    And eyesight quite keen.
Our slugger can zing
    Each pitch you may hurl.
And one other thing:
    Our slugger's a girl.

11

A BASEBALL

Stitch it.
Pitch it.
Drive it.
Ditch it.
Pound it.
Ground it.
Bounce it.
Bound it.
Bash it.
Smash it.
Crash it.
Mash it.
Hit it.
Split it.

Been there.
Did it.

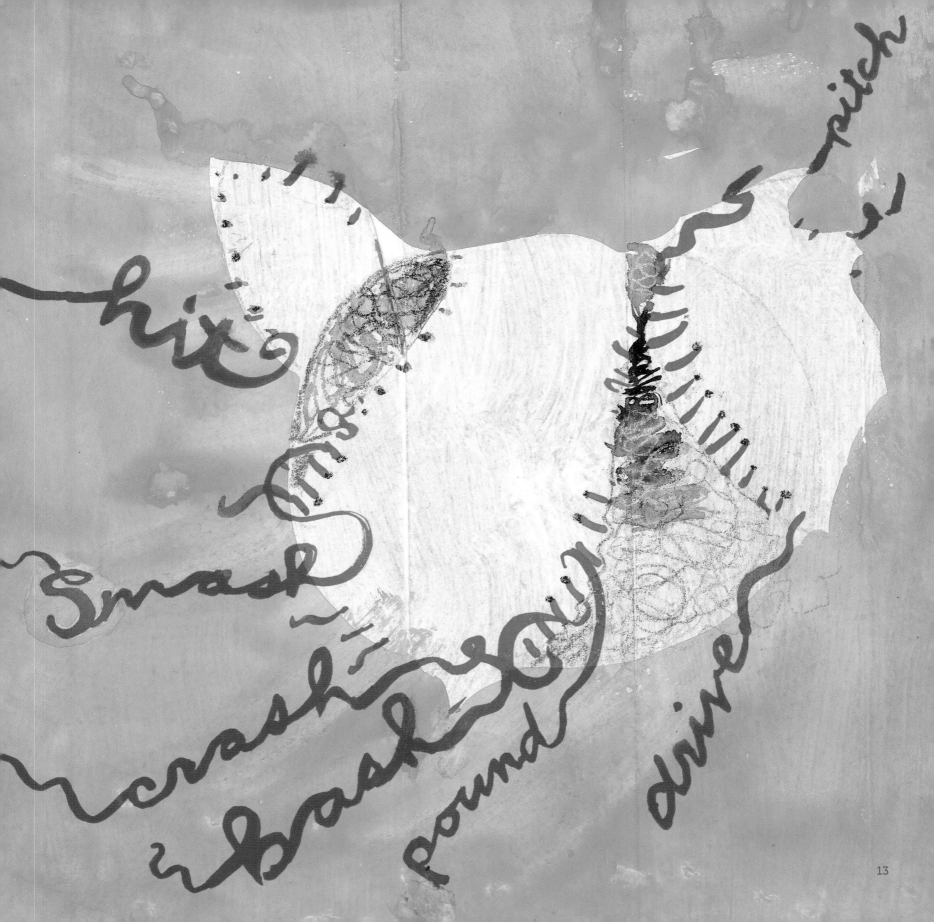

hit

smash

crash

bash

pound

drive

pitch

13

FIRST BASEMAN

First base is the worst base:
I never can sit still.
First base is the worst base:
I never get to *chill*.
First base is the worst base:
I never get to rest.
First base is the worst base.
But I love first the best.

BASE STEALER

With greatest greed
I take my lead.
My greatest need
Is speed.
I steal your base
Before your face.
You blink—
I've done the deed.
My feet are fleet.
Each steal is sweet.
I've even stolen home.
And you should know,
Before I go,
That I will steal this poem.

RIGHT FIELDER

I can't catch.
I can't run.
I'm right in right field
'Neath the sun.
I can't hit.
They say I'm lazy.
But I know how
To pick a daisy.

UMPIRE

I am the umpire.
I love to wear black.
I am the umpire.
I'm under attack.
I am the umpire.
I don't wear a glove.
I am the umpire.
I'm not too well-loved.
I am the umpire.
You don't know my name.
I am the umpire.
But I rule the game.
I am the umpire.
Don't yell and don't shout.
I am the umpire.
Strike three—you're out!

SECOND BASEMAN

Second base
Is my position.
My favorite place
By my own admission.
I love to turn
A double play.
And how I yearn
To field all day.
I snatch and catch
Balls hit up the
　　Middle.
Just don't call me
Second fiddle.

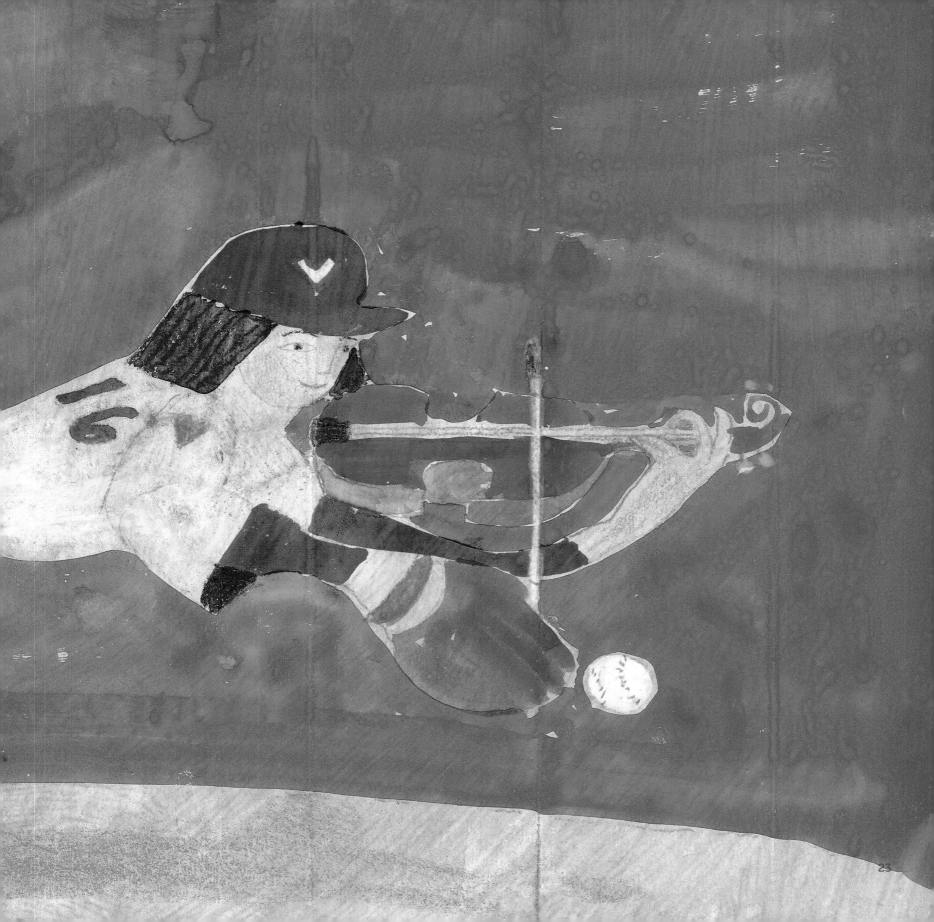

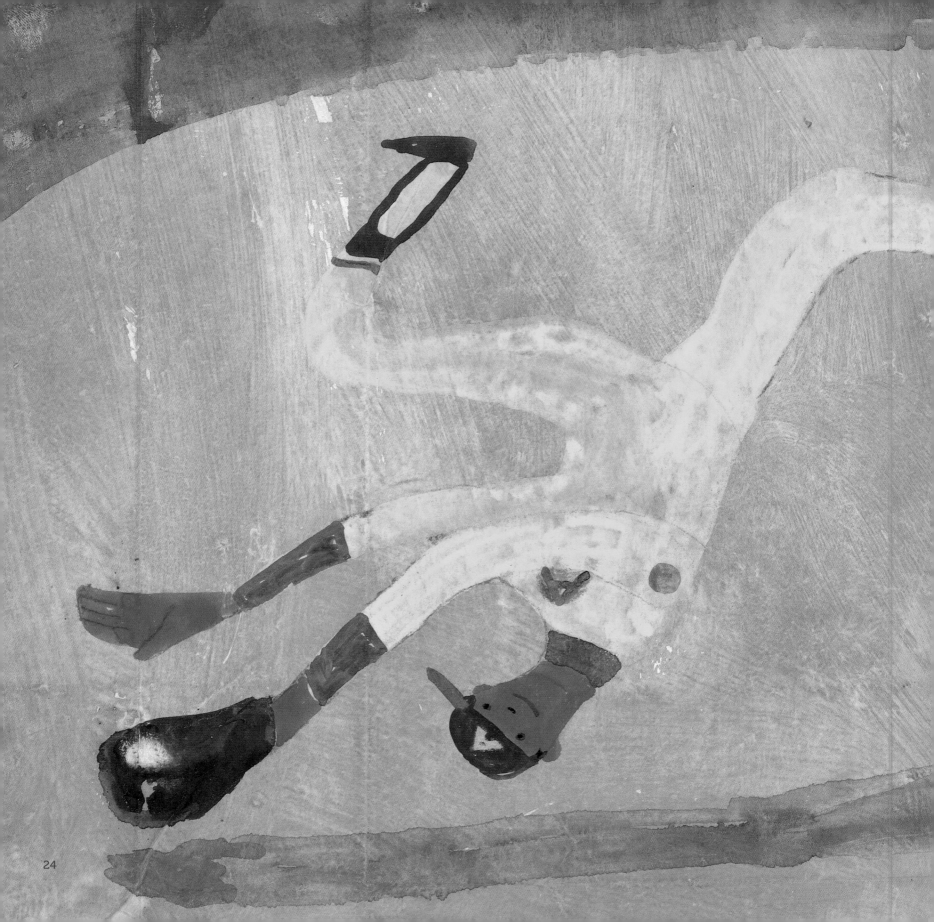

SHORTSTOP

Our shortstop isn't short.
He's tall.
He spears each
Hard-to-reach ground ball.
He *dives* for line drives.
      s for flies.
    p
  a
 e
L
Catches pop-ups
With his eyes.
With speed he leads
A double play.
Hey, shortstop—
Don't stop short today!

THIRD BASEMAN

I am the ace upon third base—
My arm is strong and steady.
For throwing runners out at first,
I'm always rough and ready.
A leopard, I leap on line drives,
Catch fly balls like a bird.
Who is the best? Who beats the rest?
Remember: Third's the word!

POEM RUN

I smashed a line drive deep to right.
It cleared the fence, clear out of sight.
I rounded the bases:
First
        second
                third
                        home,
                    and
            then
I ran *home*
And wrote down this poem.

THE SEASON IS OVER

The season is over.
The season is done.
We hit lots of homers.
We had tons of fun.
We won and we lost,
But no one's complaining.
We're counting the days
Until it's spring training.

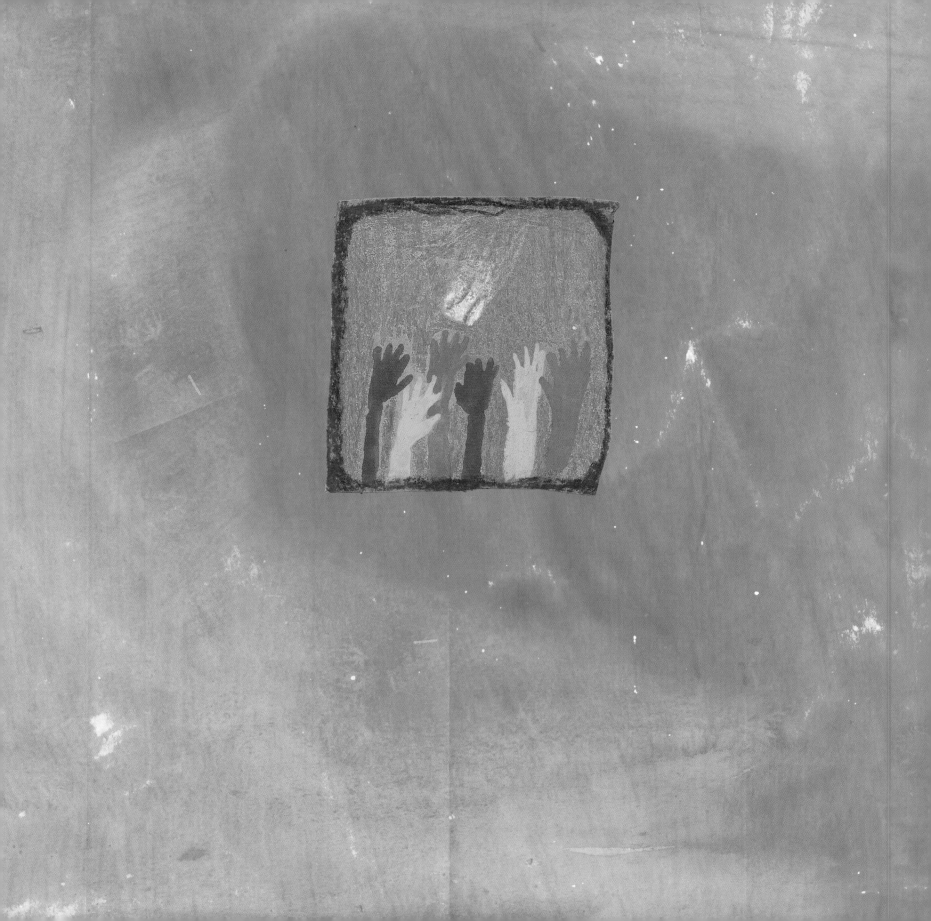